# Reflecting
on
# Leadership

by
Karin Wittenborg
Chris Ferguson
Michael A. Keller

December 2003

COUNCIL ON LIBRARY AND INFORMATION RESOURCES

## About the Authors

**Chris Ferguson** is dean for information resources at Pacific Lutheran University. Previous positions include executive director for public services of an integrated library-computing organization at the University of Southern California and director of USC's Leavey Library, which created the nation's first information commons.

**Michael A. Keller** is the Ida M. Green University Librarian, director of academic information resources at Stanford University, publisher of HighWire Press, and publisher of the Stanford University Press. Before coming to Stanford, Mr. Keller was associate university librarian and director of collection development at Yale University. He has also served as music librarian at the University of California, Berkeley, and at Cornell University.

**Karin Wittenborg** has been university librarian at the University of Virginia since September 1993. She came to Virginia after eight years as associate university librarian for collection development at University of California, Los Angeles. Before then, she held a variety of positions in the Stanford University Libraries. She spent 1980–1981 at the M.I.T. Library as a Council on Library Resources academic management intern.

ISBN 1-932326-06-5

Published by:

**Council on Library and Information Resources**
**1755 Massachusetts Avenue, NW, Suite 500**
**Washington, DC 20036**
Web site at http://www.clir.org

*Additional copies are available for $15 per copy.*
*Orders must be placed through CLIR's Web site.*

# CONTENTS

# Introduction

In one study and report after another, we learn that leadership is needed in the library profession. Yet in our many discussions of the need for better, more effective, or new-style leadership, it becomes clear that the term is not commonly defined. We all know what leadership is when we see it (or better yet, experience it), but it is terribly difficult to define.

Over the past several years, the Council on Library and Information Resources (CLIR) has tackled some aspects of leadership development. In so doing, we have called attention to the need for a greater awareness of trends and directions in higher education and scholarly communication. We have also emphasized the need to identify individuals prepared to work with the contributors to the academic enterprise to create a new system that allows scholars to create knowledge more efficiently and effectively and that enables students and other researchers to make maximum use of that knowledge.

The Frye Leadership Institute and the Scholarly Communication Institute—both successful and important programs—are designed to foster leadership development; even at these sessions, however, the personal qualities that produce leadership have been little discussed. This set of essays by three leaders in librarianship was commissioned to delve more deeply into the personal qualities of the leader.

Certainly, different individuals have vastly different styles of leading—and what they accomplish depends upon the fit of their particular skills with the needs of the institution in which they work. We asked the authors to write candidly and personally about how they developed an understanding of their own strengths and styles, what they believe leadership is, and how they apply that self-understanding to their daily responsibilities.

Selecting authors for this publication was extremely difficult, for our profession today has many outstanding leaders. Rather than attempt to identify the "best" leaders, we simply asked individuals whom we believed would be willing to help us think through the issue of leadership in truly personal terms. Each of the authors has taken a distinctly different path in fulfilling his or her leadership mandates, and all three are recognized for bringing new visions of librarianship to their work.

I am deeply grateful to these authors for their willingness to reveal themselves in this way. I believe that there is much to be learned in examining how each of them understands the role of the librarian in an institution of higher education. My hope is that these essays will result in greater self-reflection for all of us.

*Deanna B. Marcum*

## Karin Wittenborg

# Rocking the Boat

*There is nothing more difficult to take in hand, more perilous to conduct, or more uncertain in its success, than to take the lead in the introduction of a new order of things. Because the innovator has for enemies all those who have done well under the old conditions, and lukewarm defenders in those who may do well under the new.*

—Machiavelli, *The Prince*, 1532

Writing an essay on change and leadership seemed like an irresistible opportunity. I was sure it would be fun, not to mention easy. I accepted immediately, without thinking too far ahead or sorting out all the implications. In fact, this sort of spontaneous commitment has been a characteristic of my career, and it has brought about great opportunities as well as disquieting moments.

It turns out the writing wasn't so easy,[1] but it has given me an excuse to step back and reflect on the core qualities of leaders, on the advantage of an institutional culture that is open to change,

---

[1] I am indebted to Charlotte Morford, director of communications at the University of Virginia Library, who improved this essay by offering kind yet rigorous criticism as it was in progress.

*1*

and on how personal traits and prior experience have shaped the way I lead change at the University of Virginia (UVa). In articulating some of the challenges, issues, and rewards associated with institutional change, I am reminded that the rewards far outweigh the difficulties.

The leaders I most admire are visionaries, risk takers, good collaborators and communicators, mentors, and people with uncommon passion and persistence. They have personal integrity, they are assertive and ambitious for their organizations, they are optimists even in bad times, they think broadly and keep learning, and they build relationships and communities. They bring energy and a sense of fun to their work, they are opportunistic and flexible, and they are not easily deterred.

Leaders want to change the status quo. They do not seek change for its own sake, but rather to improve or create something. Leaders continually evaluate and assess their organizations with an eye toward improving them. While many administrators advance their organizations by tweaking a few things here and there, leaders aim for substantive change that introduces something entirely new or vastly improves a service or product. In short, leaders are dissatisfied with the current situation and are motivated to change it. What differentiates a leader from a malcontent is that the leader has learned and honed skills that allow him or her to move from dissatisfaction to effective action.

Achieving significant change also means rocking the boat, and this inevitably creates some degree of turmoil. Occasional or one-time leaders may be very effective in achieving change, but find the upheaval too uncomfortable or personally draining to sustain an ongoing climate of change. Institutional or personal reasons may also discourage such individuals from repeatedly initiating change. Persistent innovators accept that disruption is inevitable, have a notion about how to reduce the turmoil, and generally have strong support networks. They also had better have thick skin. In my experience, they are most likely to thrive in institutions that are entrepreneurial and flexible.

When I came to UVa in 1993, I found an institution open to new ideas. The staff—both in the library and beyond—was superb. Thomas Jefferson's presence obviously still lingers at the institution he founded. UVa is a place where entrepreneurs can flourish, where innovation is valued, and where radical change can take place. It is an institution that is traditional yet inventive.

It's often said that you cannot give a talk at UVa without quoting Mr. Jefferson. I quickly learned that it is also quite useful to invoke Mr. Jefferson when introducing significant change or seeking financial support. Fortunately, he was a prolific writer, providing innumerable quotations to support nearly any endeavor. For example, in 1810, Mr. Jefferson must certainly have been imagining the library's digital initiatives when he wrote, "I am not afraid of new inventions or improvements, nor bigoted to the practices of our forefathers. . . . Where a new invention is supported by well-known principles, and promises to be useful, it ought to be tried."[2]

Jefferson's love of books and libraries is well documented and is shared by many at the university today. Best of all, UVa President John Casteen is a humanities scholar with an unusual understanding and appreciation of libraries. So, in many ways, the institutional stars were well aligned for change when I arrived in 1993.

I did not set out to be a library director, but I have always wanted things to be better. From the beginning of my career, I have tackled the things that dissatisfy me most and tried to change them. Sometimes I have been successful, sometimes not. Sometimes my contributions were appreciated, and sometimes not. I learned gradually how to ensure that the successes outnumbered the failures. My early professional experiences shaped my thinking and behavior in significant ways. In my first library position, as an assistant to the director and deputy director of a research li-

---

[2] Letter to Robert Fulton, 1810. From *The Jeffersonian Cyclopedia*, John P. Foley, editor, 1900. Available at http://etext.lib.virginia.edu/jefferson/quotations/foley/. See entry 4042, at http://etext.lib.virginia.edu/toc/modeng/public/JefCycl.html.

brary, I had an opportunity to observe the library administration, gain an understanding of the issues they were facing internally and externally, and observe the formal and informal leadership in the organization. Many entry-level jobs narrow your horizons rather than expand them, but this one imprinted on me a broad view of the library. It also stimulated my interest in the rest of the university and in higher education in general.

Several years later, after I had moved to another institution, my boss became a role model and a mentor. I learned from her to be ambitious for the department and for the library as a whole. She thought creatively and on a grand scale, never constrained by lack of resources. Instead of being inhibited by what might be possible, she asked for what she really wanted—and often got it. She was passionately committed to her work and wanted to have fun along the way, and she made a difference at the institution. She was not a champion of the status quo.

These early experiences also convinced me of the value of collaboration. I once introduced two researchers from different disciplines who were using the same set of machine-readable data, thinking they might find common ground. They were delighted to meet, decided to collaborate, and gave me an inordinate amount of credit for bringing them together. I was immediately hooked on facilitating collaboration.

When desktop computers were still rare in libraries, I was able to secure a number of workstations for my department. In truth, I had no idea what I was going to do with them, and some of the staff were less than sanguine about the opportunities that this equipment would provide. I did have the insight to know that I wanted to share the risk and to increase the chances of success, so I divvied up the equipment with another department head. It was risk management, rather than generosity, that motivated me, but it was abundantly clear that more and better ideas came from sharing the wealth. At that point, I became a true believer in collaboration.

Having a broad vision, the guts to go after what I want, and an understanding of the power of collaboration has served me well, but this is only part of the story. As the university librarian I may be a catalyst for change, but it is the leadership at various levels of the organization that makes change happen. When I interviewed for my current position, I had been impressed by the knowledge and dedication of the library's professional and paraprofessional staff. By and large, they seemed to be open to new ideas and new ways of doing things. The personnel structure was also flexible, allowing for easy and timely restructuring when needed.

Within a week of my arrival, I realized that I had an extraordinary colleague in Kendon Stubbs, the deputy university librarian.[3] He is brilliant and analytical, innovative and inventive, knowledgeable about academia, and committed to ensuring that the UVa Library is a leader in supporting the scholarly community. Knowing that we had an opportunity to transform the library, he and I recruited our superb human resources director to the senior management team as associate university librarian (AUL) for organizational development. Over the next few years, we recruited two other AULs, building a team that has been enormously influential. We have a common vision for the library, but we bring different perspectives and strengths to our work.

One of the most valuable things our senior management team does is to rigorously examine and critique ideas, plans, and opportunities. We all have a bias for action. We have spirited and

---

[3] Kendon Stubbs had been at UVa since 1961. He started the EText Center and also Library Express On-Grounds, the free delivery of texts (print and digital) to faculty offices. He is also the founder of the Japanese Text Initiative (a collaborative effort with the University of Pittsburgh). In 1998, he received the Thomas Jefferson Award, the highest honor given by the University of Virginia. Other members of the library administration include Gail Oltmanns, who played a pivotal part as associate university librarian (AUL) for organizational development; Diane Parr Walker, formerly director of the Music Library, who is now AUL for user services and the new deputy university librarian; and Martha Blodgett, AUL for production and technology, who came to us from UVa's Information Technology department. In 2003, Kendon Stubbs and Gail Oltmanns retired. In an administrative reorganization, Hoke Perkins, AUL for philanthropy and director of the Mary and David Harrison Institute, and Charlotte Morford, director of communications, joined our team. Jeanne Hammer (currently director of facilities and capital projects) served as the library's first director of development and was instrumental in raising $37 million in the last fund-raising campaign.

sometimes uncomfortable discussions. We agree that leadership exists throughout the organization, including among the students. Good ideas come from everywhere, and one of our most important roles is to facilitate implementation of the ones that will have the most positive impact at UVa and on the scholarly community.

We can generally judge the impact because we have been seeking as much information as possible from our core audiences: faculty, students, and staff. For the past 10 years, we have been strategically collecting and analyzing data through surveys, interviews, and structured research. The data have been invaluable in guiding us toward what we must do and suggesting what we might stop doing.

We stop short, however, of letting data drive all our decisions and ideas. Some of our greatest successes have come from anticipating what might be needed or wanted, even though we had no data to support the new venture. We explore things together, even if we disagree. The library's collaborative efforts with other departments at UVa and with other entities have produced better ideas, more expertise, a broader base of support, and sometimes even more resources than would have been possible had we decided to go it alone.

But perhaps that statement needs to be qualified. Sometimes you get more resources, but you can't count on it, especially in higher education. The UVa Library has had a history of scarce resources. We have been underfunded and understaffed and have inadequate space, but we were used to that and found ways to work around it.

For example, when Kendon Stubbs started the EText Center (Electronic Text Center for Humanities) in 1992, he consolidated two collections to clear a modest room. He reallocated a single professional position, bolstered by student staff. The equipment was rudimentary. No one was demanding electronic texts in those days, but Stubbs was sure that a demand would surface when the transformational potential for scholarship became clear.

The EText Center soon garnered international attention, and we were able to secure greater institutional support along with much-needed foundation funding. Virtually all our other initiatives were started in the same way, that is, by reallocating funds and staff internally. While the library's budget is now growing, it is still modest compared to our operations and aspirations. For us, the vision and the will are far more important than the resources.

When the library started its digital initiatives in 1992, many faculty and staff, and some university administrators, questioned the investment of resources in what they perceived as a questionable venture. Fortunately, we had allies. By 1993, a number of highly regarded faculty, who were either already experimenting with digital information or could recognize its potential impact on scholarly communication, lent support and credibility to our efforts. As one of the founders of the Institute for Advanced Technology in the Humanities (IATH), an independent research center reporting to the university administration, Stubbs made sure that the institute was housed in the library. The library thus became the initial center for digital activity, and we created a community of people who shared ideas and expertise.

Now that our digital initiatives have been recognized, often imitated, and have attracted external funding, most faculty believe that we have gone in the right direction. Some remain opposed, while a few at the other end of the spectrum believe we should abandon our traditional activities.

We had, and still have, some skeptics among the library staff. At first, few people paid much attention to the digital activities that seemed to be occurring at the margins of library life. We encouraged interested staff from other areas of the libraries to volunteer a percentage of their time to work in the EText Center. There they learned about the new initiatives, acquired new skills, and augmented the center's staffing. Word started to spread among the staff and others about the digital initiatives, especially as they began to draw the attention of the press. The usual mixed feelings surfaced: pride in being considered a leader, concern about being passed by or becoming obsolete, excitement about new opportunities, and fear about competition for scarce resources.

We developed the concept of the Library of Tomorrow, or LofT, to bring together all of our activities, digital and nondigital, under one umbrella. We wanted to emphasize the integration of traditional and digital formats and services and to communicate to staff that change would be continuous.

LofT succeeded in some ways and failed miserably in others. The LofT concept appealed to alumni and many donors, especially those interested in technology. Like the staff, some were energized by the notion and eager to help advance the LofT vision in any way possible. Some of our staff, however, wanted no part of it and opted out through finding other jobs or retirement. Still others lingered in limbo. Then the state's budget crisis forced us to look hard at what we were proposing to invest in LofT and to resolve how staff were (or were not) going to be motivated by it.

Budget cuts and hiring freezes, though unwelcome, sometimes have a salutary effect. Priorities come under closer scrutiny and conflicts rise more readily to the surface when resources are in short supply. I realized that many staff did not share the administration's view of LofT as an integrated enterprise. Instead, they saw our digital and traditional collections and services as being on two separate and competing tracks. Some believed we should focus our reduced resources solely on our traditional mission; others believed we should focus them on the future.

This was unsettling news for me, but it was also critically important. It meant that I had not effectively communicated the plan for how we were going to get from today's library to tomorrow's, and that many staff did not understand how priorities were set. While I remain convinced that we are heading in the right direction, the LofT experience taught me that our planning process is not achieving everything we want it to, and that our communications program, which had been directed externally, needs a stronger internal focus. Clearly we have work to do, and improving communication will be an ever-present goal.

The LofT experience also crystallized for me what is perhaps the greatest leadership challenge: helping people thrive in an environment of constant change. This challenge is particularly acute in today's research library environment. Our staff are resilient, but many find it disconcerting to discover on a regular basis that their carefully acquired expertise has become irrelevant or is about to become obsolete.

People who thrive during periods of rapid, ongoing change tend to seek and enjoy learning. They are oriented to what the customer needs rather than to what they themselves know. Their identity is not too closely tied to a static base of knowledge and abilities. They get significant satisfaction from learning new things and delivering collections and services in new ways, but they also need compensation, recognition, and support.

As a public institution in the throes of financial cutbacks and hiring freezes, UVa has not been able to offer raises to its staff in the last three years. This can have a detrimental effect on staff motivation. Retention and recruitment of the best staff are critical to our success. Since the economic malaise has affected almost every university, as well as the commercial sector, we have been fortunate in keeping most of our staff. But we are focusing increasingly on creating an environment that will attract new staff members and encourage the best ones to stay. Such an environment offers, in addition to a competitive salary, training and educational opportunities, potential for growth and advancement, autonomy, and recognition of accomplishments. Most of our staff take advantage of our existing training programs, which draw on local, regional, and national or international experts. But we need to make significant additional investment in training and staff development.

A number of internal issues have surfaced, sometimes repeatedly, as we have implemented change. These issues include compensation, consensus, culture, control, and criticism.

First, *compensation*. As we have increased the number of staff with sophisticated technical skills, we have simultaneously created a wider gap in our salary structure. Many staff complain that traditional skills are not as well compensated as technical skills are, and they do not accept that this is a market-driven disparity. The problem is compounded by a tendency to confuse value with salary. People who are paid less often feel their work is undervalued as well. Comparing the salary of the dean of the College of Arts and Sciences with that of the football coach is the best way I have found to put this issue in context, but it does not always help.

I am often frustrated by conversations about *consensus*. Some librarians here and elsewhere believe that the word "consensus" means 100 percent agreement, rather than majority support. I think that efforts to achieve complete consensus create a barrier to change. Significant changes are controversial by nature, and they are guaranteed to provoke opposition. Discussion is essential, listening to contrary views is essential, and modifying plans on the basis of new information or perspectives is often wise. But I do not believe you can achieve 100 percent agreement on anything truly important. Having majority support is empowering and will often accelerate change. Spending too much time trying to bring everyone on board before starting, however, is a recipe for failure.

Like other libraries, UVa has experienced many *culture* clashes—far too many to enumerate. One common conflict is between the good and the perfect. I think the quest for improvement is essential, but it in no way implies a quest for perfection. In the past, libraries may have had the luxury of fine-tuning a service or product until it was (almost) perfect. The rate of change and the changing technology no longer permit this approach. Perfection is not only virtually unobtainable but often unnecessary. Settling for "very good," or even "good enough," can win the day. Nevertheless, many staff find it difficult to compromise their exacting standards.

The pace of change in academic libraries has accelerated in the last two decades and shows no sign of abating. For libraries with ambitious agendas, the change is even faster and the terrain rougher. As our responsibilities grow, it is impossible to *control*, or even know about, much that is happening in our bailiwicks. If we have good staff who exercise initiative, we may frequently be surprised by what they have achieved and how they have achieved it. Leaders throughout the organization must learn to be comfortable with exercising less direct oversight; they must focus on the goal rather than specify exactly how it is to be achieved. Chances are that the people most closely involved in a project already have a good idea of how to proceed toward the goal, even if the steps are somewhat different from those envisioned by the leader.

Leaders of change learn to be comfortable with very tenuous control, but even those who initiate change often find it stressful. I am fond of a quote from Mario Andretti: "If you think you're always in control, then you're not going fast enough." Change is exhilarating, but unsettling. I would rather surrender a great degree of control than achieve only what is possible in a slow, methodical manner.

Constructive *criticism* is invaluable when an initiative is undertaken and at any time during its development when a direction can be modified. Open and timely expressions of concern, suggestions, and alternative opinions have strengthened our operations. The changes for which the UVa Library is known have been shaped and guided by such criticism. Even when a project is completed or an initiative has become established, reassessment and criticism can strengthen an organization. Finding out what could have been done better, or what may have impeded progress, helps inform future endeavors.

What is difficult is the criticism that is not constructive. We are all familiar with the detractors who speak up only after a change is made or who work covertly to undermine the organization. As Winston Churchill said, "Criticism is easy, achievement is difficult." I don't have much patience with individuals who stay on the sidelines expressing a litany of complaints and critiques. Inevitably, anything worth doing will have its detractors, and every library has some disaffected staff. Our organizational development program has made great strides in keeping the detractors and the disaffected to a minimum. Some people have revitalized themselves by changing positions within the library, others have chosen to work elsewhere. Still others have chosen not to move. I must recognize that detractors and disaffected exist and find ways for their concerns to be heard, yet not let them undermine morale, waste too much time, or interfere with progress. I feel regret when people who could make significant contributions marginalize themselves instead.

Achieving something significant is almost always hard. Enlightened optimism gives me the confidence and courage to go forward, even in the face of opposition and obstacles. I don't like even to entertain the idea that I might fail, so I focus on how to make something happen rather than on what can go wrong. And when something does go wrong, I am eager to fix it or to inspire other people to fix it. The problem solving becomes a challenge and a game in which you must adopt a new perspective or a new strategy to win. And who doesn't like to win?

Optimism also makes me much more comfortable with taking risks. Counting on success can be a self-fulfilling prophecy. Optimism is particularly helpful in troubled times. Even when budget news is dire, I am convinced that the library can move forward, and I look for ways to turn the worst of situations to our advantage. I am always looking for victories, even small ones, that buoy our spirits and suggest better times to come. When my own optimism is shaken, I don't let on.

I say this because I believe that fearlessness, or at least the appearance of it, is another asset in achieving change. The same spontaneous commitment that has sometimes made me take jobs that were financially disadvantageous or did not have obvious career paths has given me incredible freedom. For reasons not necessarily rational, I have been only tangentially concerned with job security and therefore have done some daring things that I might not have if keeping my job was foremost in my priorities. That lack of concern, along with geographic mobility, has also made it easy for me to move out of untenable or stifling situations.

Setting priorities necessarily means that some other things do not get done. Most libraries are short staffed, and we all have limited time. In choosing the things the organization will do, some irksome problems go unaddressed or some exciting opportunities pass by. It is not always clear to staff why this happens. I believe our evolving library planning process will strengthen staff engagement in priority setting at every level and that it should clarify what will and won't get done. Of course, problems are solved and new initiatives are undertaken all the time without my involvement, but I feel some regret when those that might benefit from my attention do not receive it because I deem the outcome not to be worth the investment of time. We all make these choices—the tricky part is not feeling guilty or inadequate as a result.

We make the same choices in balancing external professional activities with institutional commitments. While I have been moderately active in professional organizations in the past, I now focus most of my energies on UVa. Because this is a place I feel passionately about and a place that is open to change, I want to accomplish the most I can. Retaining and recruiting the best and most diverse staff, providing the best services and collections to faculty and students, securing the library's financial future, facilitating innovation, improving the student experience by building and renovating libraries, and participating in pan-University endeavors continually renew my energy and commitment. It is immensely interesting and rewarding to have the opportunity to influence university endeavors beyond the library and to collaborate with other parts of the university.

I have mentioned that stress and discomfort accompany change, even when you initiate it yourself. For me, both the motivation and the rewards come from making a difference in the university. For example, faculty regularly tell us that our free delivery service LEO (Library Express On-Grounds) makes them more productive in their scholarly work and is a powerful incentive in recruiting new faculty. Our digital initiatives have brought many of the library staff into collegial collaborations with faculty and graduate students. The staff are seen not merely as technical experts but as essential partners in conceiving, designing, and implementing a project. There is enormous satisfaction in making it possible for faculty to create work that would have been unimaginable 10 years ago, to share it with a wide audience, and to ensure its preservation and availability.

Not all faculty, of course, are engaged in large-scale digital research projects, and many of them are concerned about the commitment of time that is needed to use technology. In collaboration with UVa's Information Technology department, the library has been working on ways to also help neophyte faculty who want to use technology in teaching. In their evaluations of the program, some faculty participants told us that they had conversations with graduates and students that would never have occurred in their traditional classes; others have reported that the use of their newfound skills would reshape their research. That's pretty addictive stuff.

The library is now recognized as facilitating informal interaction between the faculty and students. In 1998, when we opened the Alderman Café inside the graduate humanities and social sciences library, we had many skeptics and even a few staff resignations. Fortunately, the Faculty Senate was an eager and formidable ally, and the café quickly became a magnet for faculty as well as for students. A number of faculty now hold office hours there, and one even holds a seminar in the café. We have doubled its size and plan to enlarge it again in 2004–2005, when we will provide more seating and daily newspapers. We are working on plans for an additional café for the renovated Science and Engineering Library as well. What can be more satisfying than facilitating interaction between students and faculty and reaffirming the library as a place for intellectual discourse? Loftier goals aside, the library benefits from a percentage of the proceeds from the highly profitable café.

Undergraduates are the heaviest users of the libraries as

physical places, and the changes we have made on the basis of data and feedback from our Student Advisory Council have demonstrably improved the student experience. Recently, the vice president for student affairs told us that a consultant's report on student life had revealed that an overwhelming number of students said that the libraries were the center of their academic lives outside the classroom. It was gratifying to hear that officially, even though our students are generous in expressing their appreciation throughout the year. That finding also prompted us to collaborate on space planning with Student Affairs, and we are exploring some radical ideas. The opportunities for positive change are infinite.

Perhaps most rewarding of all is watching the library staff develop and grow. They are smart, imaginative, energetic, and service oriented. They generate extraordinary ideas, they are resourceful even in tough times, and they are outwardly focused. Their relationships within the university and elsewhere keep us better informed, more nimble in responding to needs, and more visible to the academic community. They are exercising leadership now, and they will shape the future.

The past decade at the University of Virginia has been the most engaging and satisfying time of my career. In the end, it is all about the people. I found here a university administration that was supportive and gave me a high degree of autonomy; an accomplished faculty and student body who are a pleasure to serve; a library staff whose knowledge, intellectual curiosity, and dedication are extraordinary; and colleagues in the library profession and elsewhere who inspire me. There is still much to be done. Scholarly communication will continue to change in ways we cannot yet imagine. True collaboration with other universities, especially in digital matters, is not only possible but necessary. And while budget shortfalls have prompted us to be more experimental and creative, the next capital campaign will allow me to raise funds sufficient to support our current agenda and reduce our dependency on state funds. It is one of the most significant things I can do for the library and the university.

**Chris Ferguson**

## Whose Vision? Whose Values?
On Leading Information Services
in an Era of Persistent Change

In the waning days of World War II, after years of physical deprivation and psychological terror, Viktor Frankl walked away from the daily prospect of death in a concentration camp. Later, he wrote compellingly of those horrors, laying the foundation for a new school of psychoanalysis and offering to us a framework for assessing our relationship with the world (Frankl 1963). We cannot dictate the broad outlines of our lives, Frankl writes—when and where we are born, or the elements of family, community, nation, and historical circumstance. But we *can* choose the character with which we live our lives, the moral choices and tone with which we conduct ourselves, and what we see as the purposes and goals for our lives. In the end, Frankl tells us, we are responsible for the content, if not the context, of our lives, and within this we must understand what we can and cannot change.

Leadership is about discerning what should and should not be changed. It is about understanding the interplay of self and others, and perceiving the interconnectedness of personal and organizational values. It is about self-awareness and making choices. Key to any leadership model is the mechanism for decision making—how participation is balanced with leadership, how individual vision is reconciled with other visions, how multiple decision-making processes can be reconciled within the same institution. In the end, leadership is about realization of self through service to others and the fulfillment of collective aspirations.

When Frankl walked away from his concentration camp, the prevailing leadership model in nearly all sectors of American life was that of a strong (usually male) autocrat. The 1950s and 1960s are replete with examples of strong, purposeful leaders managing largely through command-and-control methods. In the 1970s and 1980s, as government bureaucracies expanded exponentially, the number and size of educational institutions mushroomed, and corporations typically became too large to manage as personal fiefdoms, a popular alternative archetype emerged of the chief executive officer (CEO) orchestrating a large, complex bureaucracy.

As we enter more fully into a transformative era in higher education fueled by technology and characterized by the motto of 24/7, we require yet another kind of leader—one more relevant to the emerging realities of discontinuity, ambiguity, and persistent change and transition. Situations conducive to command-and-control leadership models are becoming less common, and the benevolent CEO model is becoming increasingly unwieldy. Mobility, integration, perpetual flux, nonlinearity, and visceral distrust of leaders and institutions are some of the hallmarks of the emerging environment. Stewardship rather than personal stake, calibration of multiple visions rather than imposition of one's own vision, high tolerance for ambiguity, ability to effect simplicity on the surface of complexity, and commitment to supporting both personal and organizational development are some of the hallmarks of the emerging leader for our time.

## A Personal Context
Leading organizational change for me has largely entailed helping others think and act beyond prevailing definitions of library

and librarianship, and to move toward organizational and operational realms that transcend conventional boundaries by integrating library, computing, and other academic support services within a more amorphous, evolving, responsive agency. My notions of leadership have been deeply affected by the disruption of incorporating (i.e., clumsily assimilating) information technology in libraries in the 1980s, making operational the nation's first information commons in the mid-1990s, and, over the past decade, offering leadership for the integration of library and computing within two very different university settings.

Through these experiences I have come to believe that one of the most promising leadership models for an era of persistent change is "servant leadership," as articulated by Robert Greenleaf (Greenleaf 2002). Emphasizing connections between self and organization, between listening and understanding, and between language and imagination, servant leadership places the leader at the nexus, rather than at the pinnacle, of change. It equips the leader with tools that foster empowerment and enables participants to live more comfortably and creatively with persistent change. In an era when agile response to sudden change is at a premium, servant leadership cultivates within organizations an increased capacity for efficient teamwork that uses mission as impelling force, values as cohering force, and vision as directing force—in short, the tools for effective adaptation to the discontinuities of our present environment.[1]

When I entered librarianship, I did not expect to become a leader. After several years, I began advancing through the middle reaches of organizations primarily because I was disappointed at

---

[1] Robert Greenleaf was a Quaker with strong convictions on social justice and service. His writings and many years in leadership positions with AT&T speak to the effectiveness and relevance of his ideas within a large contemporary organization. The "servant leader" might thus also be seen as the empowering leader in a learning organization. Additional attributes of the servant leader include the ability to listen to self and to others, empathy for others that reveals individual talents and insights, concern for personal and professional growth that fosters a larger sense of community, recognition of the role of steward over resources in trust from society at large, and capacity for persuasion rather than coercion.

each successive level by what appeared to be organizational constraints that impeded meaningful change. Surely, I thought, the next level will give me the wherewithal to make a difference. Only after working at some length with insufficient self-awareness or mentoring to be the kind of leader I thought I needed to be did I realize I was making the same mistakes as most of my predecessors had made. I was leading as I had been led. Only relatively recently did I learn that change is more about people than it is about organization charts and process analyses, and that to effect lasting change, I must place myself at the nexus, rather than the pinnacle, of change. To effect lasting change, I must cultivate, mentor, listen, communicate, bring together, encourage, and let go.

Librarians in leadership roles often are positioned well to apply these principles in their intersections of faculty and student service planes. We are at the crossroads of information, technology, physical space, and electronic communication. We have the traditions of personalized service, respect for individuals and their needs, freedom of access, and privacy. Our heroes include Green, Rothstein, Bunge, Battin, and Lynch. In the playing out of these values for the increasingly digital library, whatever that may be or yet become, we can make a difference in ourselves in ways that perpetuate a dynamic cycle of personal and organizational enrichment.

Frankl assures us of our capacity to shape the character of our lives and thereby to affect the course of our work. Greenleaf offers us a leadership model that draws on the power of communities to form and to act on integrated visions. Together, these two authors transform the question of "Why me?" into "Why *not* me?" and then into "Why not *us*?" Once we have posed these questions, we begin to think very differently about who we are as professionals, the connections between our personal and professional lives, and what we will do with the resources that have been entrusted to us.

## LEADER AS LEARNER

I did not see it coming. Twenty-four years, ago I became a librarian largely for altruistic reasons related to developing and facilitating access to large print collections. At that time, research libraries were formed around large physical print collections, with such services as on-site gateways (some might say guarded checkpoints) to information. A few years later, I thought I could see the future of libraries with the advent of microcomputing and a gradual transition to digital information resources within existing service frameworks. I was so wrong.

What I did not see coming was a massive and rapid shift (for an academic-library ecology centuries in the making) from print to digital information resources, from on-site services to virtual services through the network, from an emphasis on our values and visions to those of others—in short, from us to them.[2] It has become increasingly clear that there is no place in this brave new world of largely digital information services for command-and-control leadership that does not cultivate individual responsibility. The patrician CEO can at best sustain little more than a holding action when responses to external stimuli are controlled at the executive level.

Perhaps the hardest lesson for leaders of organizations these days may be that change is often far more about leading people through a transition than about changing the operations and structures around them. At some level, most of us know this intuitively, but through both positive and negative experiences I have learned that it has become necessary to take this principle to another level of understanding and practice. One must honestly listen to, draw from, and meld the values, ideals, wisdom, and aspirations of both the organization and the larger parent institution. Moreover, in order to effect lasting systemic change (rather than temporary changes that snap back into place at the first op-

---

[2] Another way to characterize this shift is from a Ptolemaic, library-centered view of the service universe to a Copernican, user-centered perspective (Ferguson 2000, 302).

portunity), it is important to focus as much on the human aspects of transition as on change outcomes.

The second-most-difficult lesson for an information services leader in our transitional era may be to internalize the need to shift the leadership perspective from one's own thinking to that of others—to calibrate one's own vision with that of the organization, the institution, and key individuals beyond, and to see through the eyes of external constituents as well as through the eyes of employees. These seem to be simple tasks, but performing them consistently requires a degree of deference, discernment, and ideational humility that many leaders seem to lack. Call it hubris, call it self-absorption, but what some know by instinct I personally have learned with difficulty: Never assume you understand the vision of the next level, or that your ideas are more powerful or better conceived than those of others. Be prepared at all times to meld your vision and aspirations into those of others, sometimes morphing your grand notions into lesser elements within a larger canvas.

Three experiences with organizational development and change have instilled in me a great appreciation for these principles. Foremost was my involvement in bringing online the nation's first information commons—essentially a major computer-user room recast in the heart of a library—in the University of Southern California's Leavey Library. Deploying a heavy concentration of computing within the heart of the library, enabling on these computers a full range of productivity and network navigation tools (at a time when access to e-mail was strongly discouraged, if not banned outright, in most academic libraries), and providing robust service support for the use of these resources had not previously been undertaken on a large scale. The presence of this massive concentration of information technology in the library demanded a reformulation of core library values.

Only by working in a highly collaborative fashion with technology-support agencies outside the library were we able to begin experimenting with integrated technology and reference-service support. Only by empowering librarians and others within the library to view our services from the perspective of our students, with a great degree of freedom to shape programs accordingly, were we able to find our way collectively into new service models that integrated library and technology-support services. In this manner, we began to transform the enduring library values of personal service and equity of access into the new values of holistic computing, core services through the network, and making the technology work for everyone—framing principles that arose only after the participating leaders placed themselves within the nexus of change (Ferguson and Bunge 1997).

After two years awash in the adrenaline rush that came with the Leavey experience,[3] I entered into the least successful yet most instructive phase of my career as a leader. I was invited to participate first in a library-wide organization redesign and then in a larger integration of library and computing within a single administrative structure. Only in retrospect did I realize that upon moving into this realm I was inhibited by my own tendency in fluid, ill-defined situations to focus inordinately on tasks and organization charts rather than on the needs of individuals and groups. I also came to realize belatedly that the executive leadership as a whole (of which I was a part) not only shared these tendencies but also failed to understand one of the basic precepts of organization transformation:

> It isn't the changes that do you in, it's the transitions. Change is not the same as transition. *Change* is situational; the new site, the new boss, the new team roles, the new policy. *Transition* is the psychological process people go through

---

[3] Leavey Library was the work of many hands and minds, so let me be clear on my contribution to the enterprise. Charles Ritcheson, Peter Lyman, Joyce Toscan, Lynn Sipe, and many others were instrumental in fund raising, architectural design, construction oversight, and broad conceptualization of the library and its central feature, the information commons. Appointed inaugural director of Leavey several months before it opened in 1994, I was charged to define positions, design services, recruit personnel, and provide general leadership for the library during its early years of operation. For a general account of Leavey after its first year of operation, see Holmes-Wong et al. (1997).

to come to terms with the new situation. Change is external,
transition is internal (Bridges 1991, 3).

The leadership group made little effort to establish a sense of
urgency, create a guiding coalition, develop a vision or strategy,
or (arguably most important) communicate a change vision.[4] A
fundamental error in the would-be integration of library and
computing was to develop a new organization chart at the executive level, announce the changes, then turn the new structure over
to the organization to make it work. In the absence of a transition
strategy, serious morale issues emerged, old resentments resur-
faced, and polarization among groups combined to allow only
superficial, begrudging changes to be made.

During these years, I lived the all-too-common experience of
bringing a set of values and a leadership style that had worked
well within a relatively contained environment into the much
larger and more complex setting of a university library system
and then of an ostensibly integrated organization of library and
computing. With considerably less internal support at either the
line or the executive level, an absence of clear internal or external
planning frameworks, and an inability unilaterally to reconcile
competing personal visions or to create an organization culture of
empowerment, the silos of library and computing prevailed more
or less as they were prior to the integration initiative.

The first seeds of doubt about my leadership style and some
of the practices of key people around me were sown with my
participation in the three-week UCLA Senior Fellows Leadership Program for librarians in 1999. There I acquired a broader
view of my profession's leadership traditions and models, greater
awareness of myself as a leader, and deeper understanding of the
need to look for external connections when developing vision
and direction for an organization. Another turning point in the

---

[4] Eight steps for successful organization transformation are defined and
explored in the now-classic 1995 article by John Kotter: establish a sense of
urgency, form a powerful guiding coalition, create a vision, communicate
the vision, empower others to act on the vision, create short-term wins, con-
solidate and produce still more change, and institutionalize new approaches.

development of my understanding of leadership occurred during my participation in the inaugural Frye Leadership Institute in 2000. The Frye Institute was developed by EDUCAUSE and the Council on Library and Information Resources to cultivate the next generation of information service leaders in higher education. Participation in the institute enabled me to view information services from broader institutional and national perspectives. I began to look seriously at higher education in a holistic fashion and to see myself as an information services leader beyond library and computing. Taken together, the Frye Institute and the Senior Fellows program exposed me to professional values I later found expressed in Frankl and Greeenleaf in ways that affect me personally as well—principally, the values of choice, engagement, service, and fulfillment.

Before moving from the idyll of Leavey to the challenges of the larger, more entrenched, and only lightly charted territory of integrating library and computing organizations, I should have taken a Frankl moment to assess what could and could not be changed within these systems. A Greenleaf litmus test to ascertain what organizational tools and processes were already in place would have been helpful as well, followed by an assessment of the capacity for leadership and the organization to work collaboratively and humanely. Had I done so, I might well have realized the extent of discontinuity among personal, leadership, and organizational values and foreseen the likelihood of accomplishing relatively little meaningful change. Having realized this, my next steps, both professionally and personally, likely would have been very different.

My experience as a leader at Pacific Lutheran University (PLU) has been quite different, but certainly not without substantial opportunities for both professional and personal growth. Leading organizational change in a smaller university has in some respects been easier, because fewer people were involved and the union of library and computing had been in place under the same administrative umbrella for several years. On the other hand, there is a much greater expectation at PLU for communication and attention to individual and community needs from both inside and outside the organization. My principal challenges have been to begin operational integration, to revitalize the library as a presence within PLU's academic culture, and to enhance the university's capacity for teaching and learning with technology, and to do so in ways that connect with community values and aspirations.

Among my first steps at PLU was to form a leadership group representative of the entire organization. Information Resources at this institution comprises administrative computing, networking, and systems; academic user support; telecommunications; television and audio services; Web development and services; and multimedia and classroom technology support, in addition to the usual array of functions and units associated with academic libraries. I believed it was vital to begin a process of familiarization that would mitigate the operational and space boundaries that remained between library and computing, even though they were federated through the same dean and for the most part were located within the same building. Our leadership group now meets weekly to share operational highlights and to address matters of overarching interest to the organization. A planning process began in this forum, as have initial discussions on space issues (as we explore moving the main computer lab into the center of the library), a variety of fiscal challenges, and, more recently, a series of technology and renovation projects. Finding common ground within the middle reaches of an organization and understanding how similar the challenges are is a meaningful step along a continuum that we hope will lead to a deeper level of integration.

After spending several months listening to and learning from many voices throughout the university, the leadership group and I began an Information Resources planning process with a series of focused discussions, department meetings, public forums, and a leadership group retreat. In this process we paid close attention to the classic steps of organizational transformation (Kotter 1995) by articulating a sense of urgency for the need to change, maintaining a guiding coalition, and developing a vision to direct the change effort. Parallel to this, we developed the habit of communicating regularly, both in messages and open forums, and of allowing leaders to articulate and to implement these changes in ways they felt most effective.

Several months after launching this planning effort we produced a set of four documents for public review and discussion—a general plan and decision-making framework for undertaking leading initiatives plus three implementing documents that recognize the importance of sustaining momentum through specific action steps (Information Resources 2002). We accomplished this work largely through a broad-based recognition of our purpose (i.e., mission as impelling force), an understanding of common values both institutionally and operationally (i.e., values as cohesive force), and a strong sense for the need to articulate a framework for future action and decision making (i.e., vision as directing force). The chief benefits of this process have been to create a stronger sense of common purpose and direction throughout the organization, to add substance to the ideal of an integrated leadership group, to describe and accomplish a significant reallocation of human and material resources toward teaching and learning with technology, and to lay the foundation for the next phase of operational and organizational integration.

A new provost arrived just as our campus-wide strategic-planning process was moving into high gear. The arrival of the provost, coupled with the planning activity, presented the opportunity to connect Information Resources efforts more closely with other efforts around campus. In vetting Information Resources plans with the new provost, the concept of an information commons became more closely linked with campus-wide planning and melded with the provost's emerging vision of a student academic support center. This combination of a solid planning process within Information Resources and a campus-wide connection that associates it with several related programs has become the basis of an innovative concept for a Mortvedt (Library) Commons that will feature integrated library, technology, and academic support service elements.

An important dimension of leadership in a rapidly changing environment is the capacity to view organizational change and movement toward a vision as a train careening down tracks that are being placed only moments before the train speeds onto them—and to alternate frequently between the roles of train engineer and rail-slapper. The lesson here is that you sometimes don't know exactly where the train is going, when your role is that of engineer or layer of rails, or just what kind of terrain lies over the next horizon; however, by sharing a mission and vision with people at all levels you can affect (if not steer) the overall course.

The challenge for the contemporary leader in an environment of rapid and continual change, then, is truly to give herself or himself up to the vision, as well as to relinquish any effort to have direct control over the means of accomplishing it, once it has been placed into motion. At PLU, in order to form a viable vision that speaks to all constituencies, I have had to surrender the notion of an information commons as the centerpiece in a redesign of the library, along with a personal emotional attachment to a Camelot I had created around my experiences with the Leavey Library information commons nearly a decade ago. This has made it more difficult to determine precisely when I should be working as an engineer or as a rail-slapper, but it has brought with it the enormous satisfaction of witnessing the emergence of a still more powerful and galvanizing idea laden with yet more opportunities for achievement and growth by the participants. Essential to this metamorphosis in my thinking and acting has been the realization that change is about people rather than things and that I must view myself as being at the nexus rather than pinnacle of change, and the awareness that if I act on these two realizations I can find effective balance between my own views and those of others.

## THE VALUE OF VALUES

We have been hearing for some time about the coming transformation of higher education. In recent years, many of us within information services have begun to create viable frameworks for the transition from largely print to largely digital scholarly communication and teaching-and-learning environments. But relatively few of us truly understand just how massive the coming shakeout in higher education will be or the true extent and character of the restructuring that likely will occur over the next decade or so. Globalization, return to massive federal deficits, further withdrawal of federal and state funding from higher education, continuing malaise in philanthropic investing, preoccupation with national security, the ongoing struggle over matters of privacy and security, increasing demands for accountability with emphasis on assessment—all conspire to accelerate dramatically our transformation into a system of higher education restructured largely by technology, mission, accountability, and values.

Values for this new order are by no means clear. It is certain only that the values are changing and that demand is increasing for leaders who can clarify them for institutions, organizations, and even themselves. If the workplace is demanding less command and control and more inspired organizational change, if leadership now requires more personal affect than direct control, if organizational effectiveness increasingly requires movement from low-trust/high-control to high-trust/low-control models, then transparent, values-based, egoless leadership is becoming all the more important.

As leaders, we have the capacity—indeed, the responsibility—to foster creation of the values needed in our organizations. Often the most effective way of doing so is simply to get out of the way and allow the collective wisdom of the persons to whom you have entrusted these services to bring them forward. An information commons by definition possesses a hybrid, transforming character that engenders discontinuities and ambiguities. Conventional service silos and multiple service points are no longer viable, professional roles and responsibilities are considerably more ambiguous, and the convergence of information services and technologies erodes organizational boundaries. For more than a century, librarians have refined and sustained the values of personal service and equity of access, yet our new service environments demand even more. Now we must reinterpret our enduring values and formulate new ones for the next generation of information services. Finding our way to framing values in Leavey required that librarians have a considerable degree of freedom to search for new responses to new service demands. Service providers had to be empowered to do so, and leadership had to let go of direct control over that process.

A final point: Fostering change in a true spirit of discovery and receptivity to new directions can lead to unexpected results. Proliferation of the information commons concept throughout academe is both a manifestation of and an accelerant for convergence of technologies and the services that support them. The Leavey experience early on convinced me of the inevitability of the convergence of library and computing, both operationally and organizationally. Since then, integration of these agencies has been a prominent element in the professional values I espouse and an underpinning for all the organizational visioning in which I participate. It has even become a major consideration in choosing the institution with which I affiliate. The seemingly innocuous exercise of openly exploring new values for a new service arena turned out to be only the beginning of an odyssey that has led into the realm of reconceiving how organizations can be shaped to better serve the interests of the communities whose interests they serve.

## LEADER AS LEADER

Much of the latter portion of my career has been based on the premise that an effective leader enables an organization to go somewhere (presumably a good place) to which it otherwise would not have gone. The organization that has such a leader moves forward willingly and with a sense of fulfillment, having been fully engaged and appropriately inspired to become more than it was. It is not by coincidence that I have focused on the merging of library and computing as the chief arena in which to play out these values. I have done so because it is a largely unmapped frontier that readily captures the imagination and because we must find ways to populate this new world as one element in a broader-based restructuring of higher education now under way.

Frankl and Greenleaf encourage us to make choices, to serve the best interests of all, and to cultivate values that enable both individuals and organizations to realize their full potential. Taking oneself from a hierarchical role to the nexus of change entails considerable mentoring, cultivation of trust, listening, mediation, and encouragement. It requires one to see service as a transparent interface between internal and external interests. Inherent in this dimension of contemporary leadership is responsibility for the personal and professional development of individuals and, in these extraordinary times, the responsibility to explore new ways of meeting information needs for the general good of both our local and national communities.

One of my chief joys in this journey has been to witness first-hand the fruits of computing-library integration in the creation of more flexible organizations for the transition from a largely print to a largely digital world, especially the collaboration of librarians and technologists in developing networked resources, understanding user needs in holistic ways, developing new modes of assistance, and jointly instructing faculty and students. Involvement in these and similar enterprises has affected me personally through an interplay of organizational values and visioning, a life of writing and speaking, and an evolution of personal values that feed back into my professional life.

While this speaks to an intimate connectedness within the leader's professional life of values and involvement, a substantial degree of transcendence is required to lead transformation of an organization when no clear road map is available. In the case of the integration of library and computing, the leader cannot afford to be viewed primarily as either librarian or technologist. The leader must instead find a third way—one that relies on collective wisdom and the deep knowledge and expertise of others while managing still to foster a cohering vision (Ferguson and Metz 2003). This might seem contrary to some of the points made earlier in this essay, but this is precisely the paradox of leadership in the contemporary organization—the leader leads yet follows, engages yet transcends, and teaches while learning.

In this era of persistent change and transition, leadership must be experienced as striving, a tension between opposites, growth through both negative and positive experiences, and fulfillment of both organizational and personal potential. Effective leaders have a sense of calling, a vocation from which framing values are derived. The essence of an authentic leader is the feeling that she or he can make a difference and is willing to try. The effective postmodern leader thus repeatedly asks, "Why and for whom am I doing this?" As Viktor Frankl urges, we must intuitively understand what is circumstance that cannot or should not be changed and what is incumbent on us to try to change. And as Robert Greenleaf instructs, it is possible to shape our personal and professional worlds in ways that connect and enhance each other in service to the best interests of all.

REFERENCES

Bridges, William. 1991. *Managing Transitions: Making the Most of Change*. Cambridge, Mass.: Perseus Books.

Ferguson, Chris D. 2000. 'Shaking the Conceptual Foundations,' Too: Integrating Research and Technology Support for the Next Generation of Information Service. *College & Research Libraries* 61(4): 302.

Ferguson, Chris D., and Charles Bunge. 1997. The Shape of Services to Come: Values-Based Reference Service for the Largely Digital Library. *College & Research Libraries* 58(3): 252–265.

Ferguson, Chris D., and Terry Metz. 2003. Finding the Third Space: On Leadership Issues Related to the Integration of Library and Computing. In C. Regenstein and B. Dewey, eds. *Leadership, Higher Education, and the Information Age.* New York: Neal-Schuman Publishers.

Frankl, Viktor E. 1963. *Man's Search for Meaning: An Introduction to Logotherapy.* Translated by I. Lasch. New York: Simon & Schuster.

Greenleaf, Robert K. 2002. *Servant Leadership: A Journey into the Nature of Legitimate Power and Greatness.* 25th anniversary edition. Edited by Larry C. Spears. New York: Paulist Press.

Holmes-Wong, Deborah, et al. 1997. If You Build It, They Will Come: Space, Values, and Services in the Digital Era. *Library Administration & Management* 11(2): 81–82.

Information Resources, Pacific Lutheran University. 2002. Information Resources as Strategic Assets: Library and Computing for PLU 2010 and the Next Level of Distinction. Available at http://www.library.plu.edu/infores/news.cfm. Accessed September 2003.

Kotter, John P. 1995. Leading Change: Why Transformation Efforts Fail. *Harvard Business Review* 73(2): 59–67.

## Michael A. Keller

# Scattered Leaves:
# Reflections on Leadership

L
ike dry leaves in an autumn wind—some whole, some torn and in fragments, some still stem to twig, some bright, some dim—thoughts about people and experiences influencing one's performance and principles as a leader need some raking, some ordering, if they are to have any interest or use to others. Perhaps, like autumn leaves, those thoughts will find a place in a compost pit, getting purposefully recycled. Or, they might just lie moldering on the forest floor, inexorably losing their predetermined shape, surrendering constituent nutrients and fiber in the underbrush.

My thoughts on leadership are not affected by systematic study of the enormous general literature on this subject and only mildly by writings about leadership in libraries. Rather, this is an attempt to order my own thoughts about working with people, my own and their performances, and principles of leadership in research libraries. Because this assignment came from Deanna Marcum, an enormously positive influence on my own career and on the careers of many other leaders, I have concluded that there are two basic tracks or reasons one becomes a leader, both heavily qualified and conditioned by choices and luck during the course of one's professional life. One track is that determined by nature *and* nurture, the fortuitous combination of a predisposition to get to the front of the herd, almost always accomplished with support from others at the front of the herd in getting there. The other track, not one that I have experienced and thus will leave to others to write about, is having a leadership role thrust upon one. In this case, I suspect, mentors most often appear as well to assist, to inform, to guide.

## INTRODUCTION

If one were to poll faculty, librarians, library staff, alumni, deans, provosts, presidents, and other senior officers in the great research universities in the United States, university librarians would appear to be many different creatures. Executive, operating officer, master practitioner, busywork minder, advocate, task master, talking head, fundraiser, judge, middle manager, protector, confessor, key figure in the humanities community, teacher, fiscal officer, strategist, mediator, conspirator, representative, traveler, community affairs officer, deal maker, risk taker, mentor, entrepreneur, steward: all these terms, and more like them, would appear on the list of descriptors resulting from our hypothetical poll. For a few, the term *leader* would be listed as well, but those who mention that word would most likely be library middle managers and associates of the university librarian. For most presidents and provosts, university librarians are middle managers, responsible for a function thought important by some faculty while ignored by others, and for a staff revered for the immediate services it provides, not necessarily for its many and continual imaginative contributions to the processes of teaching and research. As senior officers in complex, perhaps even chaotic, academic organizations, university librarians need to be adept at taking the measure of and dancing to the tunes of deference and authority. Many faculty members have little or no comprehension of what tasks must be accomplished in research libraries to ensure that their work as teachers and scholars can be done.

With many images of what a university librarian is and does, in addition to the general lack of understanding and limited appreciation of how the great research libraries operate, the role of the university librarian as *leader* is little appreciated and understood. Yet the vigorous prosecution of varied leadership roles is precisely what defines success for research libraries in this period of genuine, pervasive, and dramatic change in the missions and methods of these invaluable institutions. And those vigorous leaders of university libraries are having a lot of fun and getting a lot of satisfaction from their multiple roles.

Some context setting is necessary. As we begin the second decade of the Age of Information, so dramatically started by the general availability of the Internet in the developed economies, it is apparent that a large overlay of new information sources and methods for information seeking and distribution supplement the traditional ones. While the Internet grew logarithmically, traditional modes and methods of publishing continued and continue yet to pump out hundreds of thousands of new titles annually. Research libraries continue to collect those traditional materials even while devising the means to deliver and support the use of digital resources. Thus, from the beginning, the "both/and" conundrum has been an apt phrase to describe the dilemma facing research libraries. That dilemma stems in part from libraries' unfunded mandate to comprehend and cope with both the traditional and the digital information arenas. It also stems from the need for library leaders to demand and foster the invention, adoption, and adaptation of new tools, methods, and mental sets that incorporate digital resources with traditional collections and services. And since there is promise—or, for some, a threat—that the digital trend might overturn the nature of libraries, there is much confusion about whether the research library of the future will be some magnificent virtual collection of sources and services, owned by no one but vital to all of humankind, whether the Information Age and the Internet will dissolve the traditional hierarchy of significance based on the size and sophistication of libraries, or whether both of these transformations will be effected.

At some level, all libraries are research libraries. However, the great research libraries differ from other libraries in terms of complexity, size, services, staffing, and even intention. This essay is written from the context of an unusual university library, Stanford, that has for 15 years combined research library functions and organization with academic computing functions and organization. This merged organization is known as the Stanford University Libraries and Academic Information Resources (SUL/AIR). Its leader, who reports to the provost, has generated some new units and acquired others because SUL/AIR and its leadership had credibility and a reputation for good stewardship of Stanford's assets. The original merger in the early 1990s brought the entire information technology apparat together with the university libraries. The newly merged organization presaged the efflorescence of the Internet and the increasing interdependence of library and academic computing services to meet the demands of a community of leading-edge scholars and their students. In 1994, the administrative computing units were split off so that they could concentrate on acquiring and implementing new administrative applications based on client-server architecture. That group, Information Technology Systems and Services (ITSS), reporting to the chief financial officer, has responsibility, in addition to administrative applications for the network infrastructure, for the 24/7 server room, and for desktop support of nonacademic applications. ITSS and SUL/AIR's leaders work closely together to ensure mutually supporting services to the Stanford community.

HighWire Press is the most public of the results of merging academic computing with university libraries at Stanford. The reengineering of library technical processes, however, preceded it, with the notable effects of speeding the delivery of newly acquired publications to readers while redeploying a couple dozen staff positions to Academic Computing. Four organizations have been added to the administrative oversight of Stanford's university librarian in the past decade. They are Residential Computing; Media Solutions, a Web site design enterprise; Stanford Professional Publishing Course, a 30-year-old continuing education enterprise; and the Stanford University Press. The latter two organizations are not integrated fully into SUL/AIR, but through projects and the sharing of resources are becoming so.

As the Information Age unfolds, what will be the changes to the appetites of research libraries for selecting materials and information for their collections? How will we provide intellectual access to collections, interpret those collections, and guide readers through the information chaos? How will we distribute information to scholars and students and provide the means to analyze, manipulate, and present information? How can we preserve collections and information for the next 10, 100, or even 1,000 years? And how might university librarians exploit the "both/and" dilemma to improve the possibilities for learning, teaching, and research? What is the nature of leadership in research libraries in this period of rapid change? Does it differ from that expressed in earlier times? These questions have only partial answers, none of them completely right and fixed, all of them contextual.

The following reflections on roles and principles of leadership in research libraries, a few of many leaves scattered over a long career at several excellent university libraries, derive from my own experience and observations since 1993 as leader of SUL/AIR, a new sort of organization with responsibilities in academic computing, libraries, and scholarly communication and publishing. The reader should remember that my use of the term *university library* refers to an organization that is involved in all of these activities, as well as in more traditional library components.

## ROLE: MASTER PRACTITIONER

Most often, one is selected to become a university librarian, a leader, in part because of demonstrated mastery of aspects or specialties in research librarianship, often as a department head or head of a subject library. In my own case, I was a music librarian and head of two prominent music libraries, at Cornell and Berkeley, before assuming the role of associate university librarian for collection development at Yale. Music librarians deal with an unusually large cluster of tricky problems in all areas of librarianship and with a wide range of media types. In addition, and much to the credit of the disciplines served, music librarians are generally regarded as colleagues in practically every sense by musicologists, music theoreticians, and practicing musicians; this builds confidence and helps ensure close working relationships in solving problems and exploiting assets.

Others become master practitioners by education and experience in other subject specialties as selectors, reference librarians, or both; as catalogers; as conservators; or as one of many other technical specialists. One characteristic of master practitioners is their ability to understand the context not only of their own work but also that of other specialists. Because of that depth of professional perspective, master practitioners are often in demand locally and beyond to work on committees. In my experience, master practitioners very well know and gain satisfaction from their roles in research and teaching. Research librarianship, in practically all specialties, is a profession that advances the work of others, often in anonymity, often displaced in time from the many points of engagement of students and researchers with collections and services. Master practitioners of research librarianship are almost always good organization people. They know how their work contributes to the academy, at large and locally, and they know how to put their organizations to work in support of the sometimes idiosyncratic needs or work habits of their clientele.

In my own development trajectory from music librarian to university librarian, I could not have had a better training ground than Yale as an associate university librarian for collection development. The gaggle of wonderful colleagues there included bibliographers and curators, heads of specialty libraries, other associates, and Millicent D. Abell, university librarian. Perhaps the most difficult role to fill in a university library is that in the penultimate layer of the hierarchy, but as an associate librarian at Yale, I developed, then polished, some essential skills and was treated to some formative experiences that eased the way into my present role at Stanford. Penny Abell was a terrific mentor, allowing plenty of scope, offering sage advice, promoting colleagues' careers, and teaching some important lessons along the way. Penny helped me develop the capacity to digest and compact complex arguments to shorter expressions in order to capture and keep the attention of provosts at key decision points. She also taught her subordinates the importance of bringing to her attention, or to that of those who reported directly to her, practically any difficulty—procedural, political, or personal. I remember well Penny's remark that if a university librarian and his or her associates cannot see a problem and understand it in common terms, that problem cannot be solved.

Some university librarians are appointed from faculty ranks and thus cannot be considered master practitioners. These people have to learn quickly and, at some basic level, must depend on what they are told by their immediate associates and other informants. Certainly, faculty members serving as university librarians are expected to represent their faculty colleagues and to protect their interests. Often they are good advocates in the offices of presidents and provosts, a circumstance always sorely needed in the history of any university library. With few exceptions, the reigns of faculty "retreads" are followed by appointments of professional librarians.

One of the truisms of leadership in the great research libraries is that there is no median or average experience. Whether one became a university librarian as a master practitioner or a converted faculty member, learning to serve in the many roles listed in the introduction takes some time, perhaps years. Because each situation is remarkably different, even a sitting university librarian moving to another university will take a year or so to learn about the vagaries of the new post. Some professional associations offer opportunities to meet colleagues and share experiences. Others focus on the new and developing realms of research librarianship. Some new university librarians find the former comfortable and the latter challenging.

It was illuminating, while developing my own skills as a librarian, to observe some poor examples of library leadership. At one institution early in my career, I noted the wreckage caused by senior library leadership whose intimates were permitted to work out their peculiar needs for dominance over subordinate staff. At another institution, the chief librarian routinely lied in private to subordinates on key matters, then reversed himself in public, probably because he could face no individual on any difficult matter. By refusing to make a key decision in the first months of his tenure, he lost all credibility as a leader with superiors and subordinates. He twisted in the breeze for years while well-qualified librarians left for better places. The judgment of the two individuals I allude to here was in each case substantially flawed. As a result of—or perhaps concomitant to—that poor judgment, their interpersonal relationships were not good, certainly not satisfying. I wonder whether others have had similar experiences. It seems to me that one should always be honest as a university librarian, but that one need not always say everything that one knows in all situations. Discretion is enormously important. Discretion gives parties to issues, whether easy or difficult, the psychological space to express themselves. Not saying everything at once or in full about one's knowledge or feelings about a matter allows others to contribute and to change their own positions. Discretion contributes to the ripening, the maturing, of people and issues.

Having credibility and experience as a master practitioner is a huge asset. Another significant asset is scholarly experience in a discipline, especially one that is heavily reliant on recorded information sources or bibliography. Yet another asset is significant experience in applying information technology to research or teaching, and, best of all, experience in developing those applications. The most important aspects of the master practitioner role in leadership are those of personal engagement and the wit to generalize from experience, then compare or contrast one's experiences with those of others to devise new concepts, methods, or approaches to research library functions.

It was marvelous to behold the polished and determined efforts of master practitioners such as Joe Rosenthal and Dorothy Gregor at UC/Berkeley and Penny Abell at Yale in dealing with enormous strategic problems in complex, often hostile, political environments. None of us is perfect, and we all have our foibles spotlighted constantly. Nonetheless, Penny, Joe, and Dorothy consistently applied their creativity and persistence across the full range of duties and situations. I continue to marvel at how they achieved so many superb accomplishments. I have tried to emulate their example in modeling and insisting upon professional performance. We in the lead positions ought to show our staff how to "play through," regardless of conditions. Our presidents, provosts, and search committees did not recruit and hire us to serve only in the easy, flush times. Nor were we hired to manage the status quo. (In any case, there is no status quo any more.) The rate of change is so great that failing to apply the highest level of professional behavior and expertise to the dramatic opportunities and problems facing us would be a terrific waste of the talents of our colleagues and of the other assets entrusted to us.

## ROLE: ADVOCATE

Advocacy in research libraries assumes many guises. Leaders are advocates for their own programs and decisions internally. Staff assess their leaders partly on the basis of the strength, logic, and credibility of their plans, projects, and programs. Leaders are advocates within the campus community—or perhaps better, communities. Leaders are advocates in the upper reaches of the university administration, and it is in this sector that the best and the worst advocacy takes place. Some strive for a series of successful "big hits," the sorts of advances in funding or program development that warrant a press release. Others strive to avoid trouble and feel best when their operations and responsibilities remain below horizons of interest; indeed, some are directed specifically to cause no trouble. A few others understand themselves as campus citizens, and as such, part of larger programmatic and budgetary processes, taking initiatives where appropriate and contributing to others when possible.

Advocacy also involves, perhaps requires, promoting and protecting the assets and values of academic institutions, sometimes in the face of competing academic and other interests. This sort of advocacy is occasioned by the never-ending ebb and flow of new program development, e.g., when a dean builds a teaching and research capacity in an entirely new field without considering the new professors' needs for library collections and services or academic computing support. Responsible advocacy also requires elevating awareness of the serials crisis to the faculty and the administration with the intention of fomenting effective action.

"Confuse 'em or convince 'em" was the motto of one respected library leader. He was referring to the pleasant duty of speaking to alumni and friends of the university about libraries, academic computing, and scholarly publishing. It can be extraordinarily difficult to present the salient features of our complicated academic information realms to a well-educated, but nonacademic, audience. And yet, if one can do this well—concisely and without jargon—both the larger institution and the library benefit. There are many audiences for library advocacy, some less obvious than others. One characteristic of the great leaders of university libraries is the ability to communicate succinctly and clearly to members of the public, as well as to their subordinates and superiors. The ability to speak to numerous groups of varying degrees of understanding about what goes on in research libraries and to gather one's thoughts instantly for impromptu interactions, as well as to develop carefully considered presentations, is another aspect of raking together quite scattered leaves.

## ROLE: STEWARD

Stewardship is an active role requiring ongoing consideration of how to invest one's institutional assets to best effect. Those assets include staff, money, facilities, time, one's own attention, institutional reputation and credibility, collections, and physical assets—facilities, information technology equipment, vehicles, and so forth. Stewardship, particularly in the great research libraries, should include engagement with the major institutional issues of the time. Currently among the great stewardship issues are those of exploiting the capabilities of information technology to improve scholarship and teaching. Also, and more sinister, is the issue of overspending on scientific, technical, and medical journals, which imbalances the range and depth of library collecting and library services. Perennial stewardship issues are those of:

- collecting, i.e., bringing in the information resources needed now, while also serving as cultural custodians;
- providing intellectual access, not just with traditional cataloging and indexing, but considering new approaches and technologies;
- deploying and fostering new information resources and academic computing applications, and the means of using them;
- distributing information; and
- preserving for future generations the information and sources we collect and apply.

Library stewardship is most effective when exercised by staff at all levels. Rather than allowing every staff member to see herself or himself as owner of a particular facet of work, we should encourage all staff to understand themselves to be contributing to the larger missions of the organization and the university. If that sort of broad ownership of the institutional mission is accepted, then adopting and adapting new methods is much easier. It also leads to greater creativity among staff members. As the strictures of our traditional guild mentality are released and staff have the satisfaction of engaging personally in the question of "How can we improve?", they begin to internalize reengineering and to think of it as the measure of success. Publicly rewarding creativity and stewardship by individuals and groups is a necessary and joyous stewardship responsibility of the senior-most leader.

Some acts of stewardship, such as stewardship of one's staff, require tremendous patience and forbearance. If one hires and promotes well, then one owes staff the space to achieve and develop. University librarians, like many other library staff, come by information about other people that demands extreme discretion. One learns to overlook certain behaviors, to hold closely some of what one sees and hears, and not to base policies on individual issues or prejudices—one's own or those of others. The times that I have failed in this regard have given me anguished moments and memories. On the other hand, the pleasure and the experience of the collective mastery of leading wonderfully complicated and constantly evolving organizations is deeply satisfying. In observing the expertise and subtlety expressed constantly and in so many different ways by my Stanford associates, I take pride in the fact that I appointed and promoted them. That same pride, as well as similar gratification, applies to the entire SUL/AIR staff at Stanford. They truly are an army of generals. Assembling, coaching, and leading a staff of such accomplished people is a special skill. One does not undertake leadership to make staff happy as a first principle, but when one finds a happy staff—happy in their work and in their collective accomplishments—one has also found an effective, if not necessarily highly visible, leader.

Library leaders who ignore stewardship—or regard it only superficially—fail to measure the costs and benefits of their commitments, never seize the nettle of change, and are thereby condemned to irrelevance. There is a kind of herd mentality in certain circles of library leadership, in which self-congratulation for half-measures in addressing huge problems and opportunities is common. An easy way to spot this behavior is to watch for press releases announcing unrealized programs and progress not yet actually made or made in tiny steps. A characteristic of this collective unconsciousness is the failure to analyze and review investments, programs, and failures, and the lack of assessment of costs and benefits.

## Role: Judge and Power Broker

The daily decisions of university librarians shape, as ripples in a pond or puddle, the activities of the staff and, through them, services to the readers. University librarians concerned about making the best use of and conserving their own energy and time wisely delegate authority to the lowest-possible level appropriate for that power to be applied. And, for me, one most important principle is to make individuals responsible for functions, units, programs, and projects. Part of that delegation of authority is to consult as needed with experts and affected parties. The use of the hierarchy of authority to efficiently apply judgment and oversight is important, too. While many berate their superiors for adhering to any hierarchy and some libraries employ "first-among-equals" fantasies of management, research libraries with efficient and clearly known tables of organization that accurately reflect power relationships generally have productive and happy staffs. Part of the effective delegation of authority and resources is making sure that those putting those assets to good work receive public and private praise. They, not the university librarian, should get their names in the campus paper.

In many university libraries, but not at Stanford as I experience it, staff time and expertise are heavily invested in ongoing and tedious consultative processes. Consultation among experts and managers is almost always useful in operations, especially as new projects, programs, and opportunities appear. However, the pervasive use of committees cutting across hierarchies in libraries—to masticate everything from the minute to the monumental—is wasteful of time and reputation. The leader must take responsibility for judgment and the exercise of proper authority; to pretend (or worse, to behave) otherwise through universal discussion is evidence either of cowardice or deception.

Certain judgments, especially those of recruiting, retaining, training, and mentoring high-quality professional staff, should be made with the advice and concurrence of carefully constituted search committees and immediate supervisors and directors. However, for that advice to be most useful, I insist on meeting almost all candidates for professional positions in my organization before receiving advice on approving an appointment. One needs to know, at least at some superficial level, the person about whom the advice is offered.

Another important requirement for a good leader in a university library is that of insisting that responsible managers raise, discuss, and resolve their differences directly as often as possible. This requirement demands communication, often face-to-face, determined coordination, and professional cooperation. Encouraging the surfacing of issues, while requiring maturity from staff in dealing with disagreement, is a key behavioral characteristic of successful university librarians, ones who motivate staff to improve constantly as well as always to enjoy their work.

Delegation of responsibility should be accompanied by the delegation of authority and assets to accomplish the assigned and accepted tasks. Librarians have not always been especially successful in honoring this principle. All librarians and information technologists are managers of assets. Given scope, power, and assets, each can accomplish worlds more with the trust implicit in such delegation than he or she will when delegation is incomplete, fitful, or limited.

## Role: Mentor and Colleague

Among the many pleasurable roles of a leader is that of recruiting and hiring good people and then helping them achieve their own career goals as well as institutional goals. This is a sort of raking together scattered leaves too. It is one of the most important roles of a university librarian, because the work of the university libraries is done by others: professionals, paraprofessionals, and students. I see the work of a university librarian as very similar to that of an orchestra conductor who is a master of one, or perhaps a few, instruments, but not of the entire complement of the symphonic ensemble. In the most accomplished orchestras, the conductor does not need to tune individual instruments and does not have to instruct a player how to produce a particular note. Instead, the conductor focuses on making music, shaping phrases, and integrating the efforts of the various sections to realize the composer's intentions. As one who has been lucky to work in four university libraries with superb staffs—say, the equivalent of the members of the San Francisco Symphony—I have experienced the incredible, if slow-moving, power of communities of specialists working together not only to serve their academic colleagues very well but also to create new opportunities for scholarship and teaching. This has been especially true at Stanford, where much of my effort has been focused on coordinating and encouraging, rather than directing.

One shapes the staff of large and advanced research libraries over time. Thoughtfully rewarding outstanding efforts and attainments is as important as is careful and patient counseling and remediation. Letting colleagues try new methods, develop collections and services according to their own best judgments, and take responsibility for internal and external relationships has proved repeatedly to pay off. Suggesting, gently shaping, and urging independence within context is the role of the leader in what I like to refer to as an "army of generals." As noted earlier, selecting, mentoring, and promoting key staff are among a leader's most important functions. It is essential, therefore, that the university librarian be directly involved in interviews and that he or she approve every hiring and promotion recommendation. It is equally important that the university librarian review and lead others to review errors in hiring and promotion. Over time, a couple of fundamental truths emerge. First, no one is perfect. Second, in an organization that values mentoring and collegiality, most colleagues are sufficiently forgiving of mistakes that the web of relationships necessary to provide services in large and complex research libraries is rarely torn.

It is failure that burns, despite the lessons each failure teaches. How can an entire interviewing team, the recommending officer, and I have missed the obduracy in someone's character that precluded her ability to adapt, to grow, and to learn professionally? Did one make successive errors in accepting the rosy-hued estimates of performance from an immediate subordinate about a staff member further down in the hierarchy, thus allowing others in the organization to lose hope for change and improvement? What are the techniques of provoking thought and consultation that might bring disputing parties to the point not just of accommodating one another on a particular matter but also of valuing their differences and perspectives? No one fails alone in an organization such as a research library, but the leader needs to understand how people fail and how to help them succeed. However, when failure is profound and not susceptible to remediation, then a good leader uses the tools available to remove a poorly performing staff member. Confronting poor performance and working on it, including dismissal, if necessary, reinforces the enormous contribution made to research library operations by the vast majority of their staff. Outstanding performers know when a coworker is not performing adequately, and they appreciate the leader who identifies, then works quickly to correct, poor performance or, if this is not correctable, removes the poor performer. Success in leadership is usually, perhaps always, the product of successful mentoring. This may be the real benchmark, the real legacy, of the library leader: the quality, integrity, and success of the colleagues whose own careers as leaders were influenced for the better through a mentoring relationship.

## Role: Strategist, Risk Taker, and Innovator

The role of strategist or strategy developer is often uniquely that of the university librarian. All subordinate to that position are involved in specific operational responsibilities, including managing others. Some issues, such as building or refurbishing facilities or acquiring special collections, require 50- or 100-year time horizons. Others, such as adopting new technologies, have much shorter horizons, perhaps five years or fewer. Some issues demand leaps of faith. For instance, in digitizing books or archives, one can estimate whether the digital versions will be of immediate utility for academic purposes, but one must also imagine that there will be techniques available within a few years to migrate the digital versions from one format to another and to store them in a securely operated digital repository. Equally, one must evaluate strategically experiments and accomplishments made elsewhere. What is supportable? What is scalable? What company or line of products and services is likely to stay in business long enough for the library's purposes? What investments of Stanford's assets—its staff, one's own time, money, facilities, or good name—will pay off for Stanford? Tending the strategic, while meddling only when necessary in the tactical, the essential day-to-day work of the university libraries' staff, is a key responsibility of the leader.

Fortunate is the university librarian who has the encouragement and expectation of the president and provost to take risks, to exploit according to his or her own best judgments the Internet and information technology in general, and thereby to serve imaginatively the campus community. All faculty members appropriately regard themselves as independent entities, suns in their own solar systems, devising ever-better courses and lectures and conducting research. In this context, the librarian's key responsibility is to constantly balance and rebalance library and academic computing resources so reliable and consistent services are offered. To do so, he or she must take risks to experiment and make use of the new technologies so that the information and services underpinning research and teaching at institutions of higher education of all sizes constantly advance and improve.

One question that we ask ourselves repeatedly is how we can make Stanford distinctive in the quality and extent of our services and information resources. Because presidents Gerhard Casper and John Hennessy, along with provosts Condoleezza

Rice and John Etchemendy, have expected and valued innovation in Stanford's libraries, devising and investing in a number of risky propositions has been relatively easy. Among the risks taken with their blessing over the past decade, those that realized huge returns on initial investment were as follows:

- HighWire Press (http://highwire.stanford.edu)
- LOCKSS (Lots of Copies Keep Stuff Safe), the software application supporting the operation of local network caches of e-journals and other genres (http://lockss.stanford.edu)
- Technical Services Re-engineering (http://library.stanford.edu/depts/diroff/ts/redesign/redesign.html)
- Rehabilitating the Bing Wing of the Green Library for reader and particularly networked services (http://library.stanford.edu/depts/green/bingwing.html)
- Institute for 21st-Century Librarianship (http://institute21.stanford.edu)
- Digitization of the Archive of the General Agreement on Tariffs and Trade (http://gatt.stanford.edu)
- Academic Technology Specialists Program (http://acomp.stanford.edu/atsp/)
- CourseWork, a course-management system

Major acquisitions involving risk included the Allen Ginsberg Archive, the William Saroyan Archive, the Samson/Copenhagen Judaica Collection, the Gustave Gimon Collection on French Political Economy, the R. Buckminster Fuller Archive, the Southern Pacific Railroad Archive, the papers of numerous luminary writers and artists in the American avant-garde and the Mexican-American community, and many others.

Finally, we have undertaken activities such as the following:

- expanding the map and GIS services (http://gis.stanford.edu/)
- considering a joint venture with a commercial paper-preservation company
- requiring the development of Web-based synthetic guides to the literature and resources of numerous disciplines.

Stanford's examples of risks taken and investments returned have required, in practically every case, some diversion of resources from traditional programs and pursuits in the university library. For any risk taken, some staff and faculty might object on the grounds that their favorite interest was not going to get as much support as they believed it deserved. One of the functions of leaders of university libraries is to take such risks and to expose themselves and their decisions to criticism and rebuttal for the sake of strategic developments.

## CONCLUSION

The metaphor of raking scattered leaves is meant to suggest the odd feeling I often have as Stanford's university librarian—in dealing with so many agenda items and so many positive developments, in weighing and selecting possibilities for attention and investment, and, frankly, in confronting the 5 percent of this work that is truly difficult and occasionally quite challenging on a personal level—that this is the best work in the university, with a bouquet of possibilities librarians have never had before. In selecting only a few of the many roles university librarians play, I do not mean that the other roles are not as important, but that these are ones I find most meaningful at this stage of my own development and at the present state of research librarianship as a profession, as a craft, as the practice of an art.

Key roles of the university library, part and parcel of the academic processes of the university itself, are to figure out how to improve, to stay current, and to exploit new opportunities in each of the library's functions: collecting, describing, interpreting, disseminating, and preserving. At the strategic level, this is the work of library leaders. It is good work, socially useful work, and immensely satisfying work. Those who do not awaken every morning eager to undertake this work need not apply.